Growing Older

by Margie Burton, Cathy French, and Tammy Jones

I was so, so little when I was
a baby. I could not see
much with my eyes. I could
not talk. I could not walk. I
could cry. I had to
be fed by Mom or Dad.

At Birth: "I could not do much by myself."

I needed to be washed and cleaned.

I needed to be warm and dry.

I needed love.

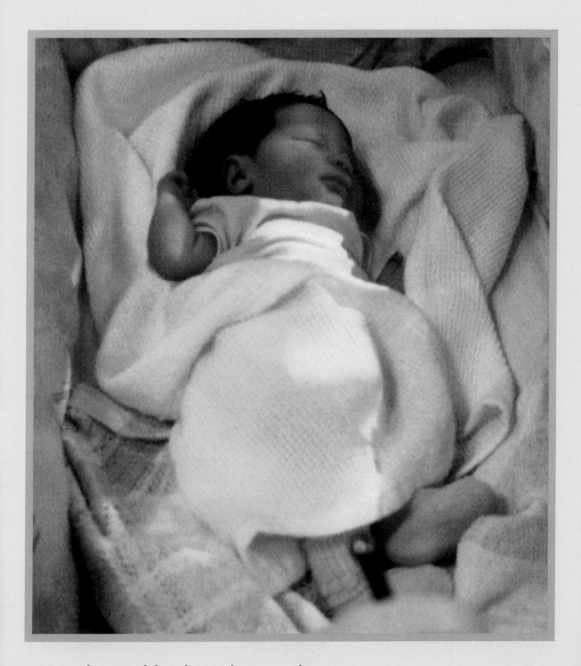

At Birth: "I liked to sleep a lot."

I was older when I was two.
I could walk. I began to talk.
My mom and dad would know
what I said. I would know
what they said to me.

Age Two: "Drink!"

Age Two: "Book, mine."

I could play when I was two.

I could get around by myself.

I could go fast!

I could jump, too! I could
eat by myself.

Age Two: "This is good!"

Age Two: "I can do it myself!"

I was older when I was four. I
could tell a story from my book.
I could sing my story, too.
I could talk and say many things.
My mom said that I talked
too much!

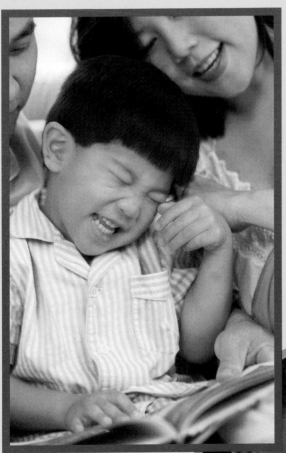

Age Four:
"I like to read my book!"

Age Four: "I like to talk!"

I could run and jump when
I was four. I could play
and do what I could not
do when I was little. I
could draw and write.

Age Four: "I can write my name!"

Age Four: "I am getting older every day."

Now I am older. I
can go to school. I can
read and write and paint.
I can ride a bike by myself.

Age Six: "I like to go fast on my bike."

Age Six: "I can work with my friends at school."

It is fun to be six. I will get to do new things when I am older.

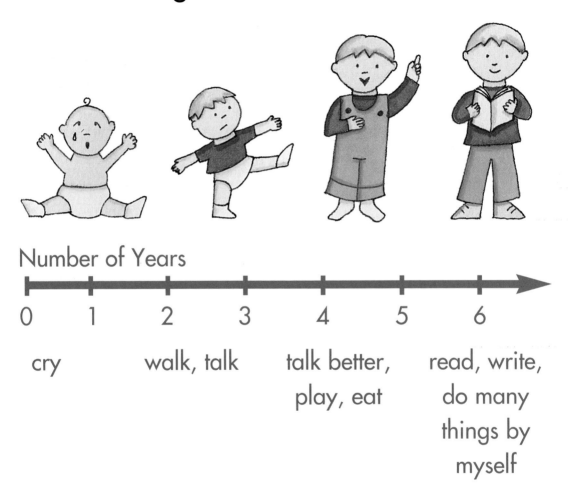

Number of Years

0   1   2   3   4   5   6

cry   walk, talk   talk better,   read, write,
                          play, eat   do many
                                         things by
                                         myself